Adjectives

Across

2. Showing courage, fearlessness, or determination in the face of danger, difficulty, or adversity. Being brave means having the strength to confront challenges, take risks, or stand up for what is right. It involves a willingness to face fears and overcome obstacles without backing down or giving up.

7. Pleasing to the eye or aesthetically attractive. Beauty can refer to the physical appearance of a person, object, or nature, as well as qualities such as grace, harmony, or elegance. It evokes a sense of admiration, appreciation, and delight. Beauty can be found in various forms, including art, nature, and the inner qualities of individuals.

8. Having the ability to produce or invent something original, imaginative, or artistic. Creativity involves thinking outside the box, expressing ideas in unique ways, and solving problems in innovative and unconventional manners. It encompasses various domains, such as art, music, writing, and problem-solving, and it allows for self-expression and the exploration of new possibilities.

9. Showing benevolence, generosity, or compassion toward others. Kindness involves acts of empathy, understanding, and consideration for the well-being of others. It can be expressed through gestures, words, or actions that promote harmony, help those in need, or foster positive relationships. Kind people are often seen as caring and supportive.

11. Causing laughter or amusement; humorous. Something or someone that is funny can make

Down

1. Pleasing to the eye or aesthetically attractive. Beauty can refer to the physical appearance of a person, object, or nature, as well as qualities such as grace, harmony, or elegance. It evokes a sense of admiration, appreciation, and delight. Beauty can be found in various forms, including art, nature, and the inner qualities of individuals.

3. Causing enthusiasm, anticipation, or thrill. Something that is exciting generates a sense of excitement or interest. It can be related to thrilling experiences, engaging activities, or events that evoke a sense of anticipation and joy. Excitement often brings a surge of energy and a desire to actively participate or engage in the experience.

4. Showing a warm, amicable, or welcoming attitude toward others. Friendliness involves being sociable, approachable, and kind-hearted. It promotes positive interactions, openness, and the willingness to build connections and friendships. Friendly individuals often create a pleasant and inviting atmosphere around them.

5. Feeling or showing pleasure, contentment, or joy. It is a positive and cheerful emotion that can be expressed through smiles, laughter, and a sense of well-being. Happiness is often associated with favorable circumstances, fulfilling relationships, or enjoyable experiences.

6. Having a pleasant taste or flavor that is highly enjoyable. Deliciousness is associated with food or drinks that are savory, sweet, flavorful, and satisfying to the senses. It can evoke a sense of pleasure, indulgence, and

people laugh or smile. It involves cleverness, wit, or the ability to create comical situations or jokes that evoke a sense of humor. Funny things or situations often bring joy and light-heartedness.

13. Full of colors, bright hues, or vibrant shades. Colorfulness can refer to the visual appearance of objects, images, or scenes. It evokes a sense of liveliness, variety, and visual appeal. Colorful things often bring joy, creativity, and visual stimulation to the observer.

15. Having physical power, muscular strength, or resilience. Strength can also refer to mental or emotional fortitude and the ability to withstand challenges or difficulties. Strong individuals possess determination, endurance, and the capacity to overcome obstacles. They can inspire others and exhibit confidence in their abilities.

16. Having intelligence, quick thinking, or cleverness. Being smart means having the ability to learn, understand, and apply knowledge effectively. It involves critical thinking, problem-solving skills, and the capacity to make wise decisions. Smart individuals are often seen as intellectually capable and resourceful.

satisfaction when consuming something that is delicious.

10. Having a strong desire to learn, discover, or explore. Curiosity involves inquisitiveness, a thirst for knowledge, and a sense of wonder about the world. Curious individuals ask questions, seek information, and eagerly engage in new experiences or ideas. Curiosity drives exploration, creativity, and intellectual growth.

12. Moving or acting with great speed or quickness. Fastness can refer to physical movements, processes, or the passing of time. It can evoke a sense of swiftness, agility, or efficiency. Fast objects or actions are often associated with rapidity and the ability to cover a distance or complete a task in a short amount of time.

14. Feeling or showing sorrow, unhappiness, or grief. It is a negative emotion that can be expressed through tears, a downcast demeanor, or a sense of loss. Sadness can be caused by various reasons, such as disappointment, separation, or the experience of unfortunate events.

Adverbs

Across

1. Doing something without making any sound or noise. Moving or acting in complete quietness. It is the opposite of being loud or noisy.

3. Speaking or acting in a sincere, truthful, and trustworthy manner. Being honest and having integrity. Telling the truth and not deceiving others.

4. Performing an action with elegance, poise, and smoothness. Moving or behaving in a graceful manner. Having a sense of beauty and refinement in one's movements.

Down

1. Moving or doing something at a relaxed or leisurely pace. Taking time and not rushing. It is the opposite of being fast or quick.

2. Proceeding with care, paying attention to potential risks or dangers. Being careful and mindful of one's surroundings. Taking steps to avoid accidents or mistakes.

6. Producing or speaking with a high volume or intensity. Making a sound or expressing oneself in a loud manner. It is the opposite of being quiet or soft-spoken.

5. Expressing anger or frustration through one's behavior, tone of voice, or facial expressions. Feeling and showing strong displeasure or irritation. It is the opposite of being calm or peaceful.

11. Demonstrating patience and endurance in waiting, dealing with difficulties, or achieving goals. Tolerantly enduring delays or challenges without getting frustrated or annoyed.

12. Engaging in an activity with a sense of fun, amusement, and lightheartedness. Acting in a cheerful and lively manner. Having a playful and joyous attitude.

13. Doing something in a calm and gentle manner without making much noise or disturbance. Being quiet and not talking loudly. It is the opposite of being loud or noisy.

15. Doing something with joy, pleasure, and a positive attitude. Feeling happy and expressing happiness while doing an activity. Being cheerful and content.

7. Performing an action with caution, precision, and attention to detail. Taking care to avoid mistakes or accidents. Being mindful and attentive.

8. Doing something with joy, pleasure, and a positive attitude. Feeling happy and expressing happiness while doing an activity. Being cheerful and content.

9. Performing an action at a fast pace or with swift movements. Acting promptly or without delay. It is the opposite of being slow or taking a long time.

10. Doing something in a soft, mild, or delicate manner. Acting with kindness and tenderness. Handling things or interacting with others in a gentle way.

14. Approaching something with enthusiasm, anticipation, or eagerness. Having a strong desire or interest in an activity. Being excited and willing to participate or learn.

After-school Activities

Across

2. Engaging in physical activities and team sports such as soccer, basketball, or volleyball. Sports promote physical fitness, coordination, teamwork, and sportsmanship. They provide opportunities for exercise, skill development, and social interaction with peers.

3. Learning basic programming concepts and creating simple computer programs or games. Coding activities develop logical thinking, problem-solving skills, and computational thinking. They introduce children to the world of technology and foster creativity through designing and coding their own projects.

6. Learning and practicing basic cooking skills and recipes. Cooking activities promote independence, creativity, and an understanding of nutrition and food preparation. They can help children develop a sense of responsibility and encourage healthy eating habits.

9. Engaging in various creative activities such as drawing, painting, and sculpting. Art allows children to express their creativity, explore different mediums, and develop their artistic

Down

1. Learning about photography and capturing images using cameras or mobile devices. Photography encourages observation, creativity, and storytelling through visual images. It allows children to document their surroundings, express their perspectives, and develop an appreciation for aesthetics and composition.

3. Engaging in various craft activities, such as paper crafts, origami, or jewelry making. Crafts stimulate creativity, fine motor skills, and spatial awareness. They encourage children to explore different materials, textures, and techniques to create unique handmade items.

4. Participating in theatrical activities, including acting, improvisation, and role-playing. Drama encourages creativity, self-confidence, and communication skills. It allows children to explore different characters, emotions, and storytelling techniques while fostering teamwork and cooperation in group performances.

5. Engaging in activities related to planting, nurturing, and caring for plants. Gardening teaches children about nature, the environment,

skills. It can be a source of relaxation and a means of self-expression.

10. Playing the strategic board game of chess. Chess enhances critical thinking, problem-solving skills, and concentration. It teaches children to plan ahead, analyze situations, and make strategic moves. Chess can be played individually or competitively, providing mental stimulation and fostering patience and perseverance.

11. Engaging in activities related to building and programming robots. Robotics activities develop logical thinking, problem-solving skills, and teamwork. They introduce children to engineering principles and technology, fostering creativity and innovation through designing and programming functional robots.

13. Spending time reading books, magazines, or online articles. Reading enhances vocabulary, comprehension skills, and imagination. It broadens knowledge, sparks creativity, and fosters a love for literature. It can be done individually or as part of a book club or reading group, allowing children to discuss and share their thoughts on different texts.

14. Participating in various dance styles such as ballet, hip-hop, or contemporary dance. Dance promotes physical fitness, coordination, rhythm, and self-expression. It allows children to explore movement, develop confidence, and experience the joy of creative expression through dance routines and performances.

and the importance of sustainability. It provides opportunities to learn about different plant species, gardening techniques, and the rewards of cultivating and observing plants' growth.

7. Exploration Exploring and appreciating nature through outdoor activities such as hiking, nature walks, or camping. Outdoor exploration promotes an understanding of the environment, biodiversity, and the importance of conservation. It allows children to connect with nature, experience outdoor adventures, and develop a sense of responsibility towards the natural world.

8. Participating in musical activities, such as singing, playing instruments, or listening to and appreciating different genres of music. Music helps develop an appreciation for rhythm, melody, and harmony. It can also be a form of self-expression and a means of connecting with others through collaborative performances.

12. Exploring scientific concepts through hands-on experiments, observations, and investigations. Science activities encourage curiosity, critical thinking, and problem-solving skills. They provide opportunities to learn about the natural world, conduct experiments, and develop a scientific mindset.

Animals

Across

2. A small, carnivorous mammal that is often kept as a pet and is known for its independence, agility, and hunting skills.

4. A highly intelligent marine mammal with a streamlined body, known for its playful nature, acrobatic swimming, and communication abilities.

6. A massive mammal with a long trunk, large tusks, and floppy ears, known for its intelligence, social behavior, and iconic appearance.

10. A highly intelligent and agile primate that typically lives in trees, known for its playful behavior, dexterous hands, and expressive facial expressions.

11. A small, bushy-tailed rodent that is often found climbing trees and gathering nuts, known for its quick movements and ability to store food for winter.

13. A tall, long-necked mammal with a unique spotted pattern and an elongated body, known for its graceful gait and ability to reach high foliage.

14. An insect with delicate, colorful wings that undergoes metamorphosis, known for its graceful flight, pollination role, and symbolism of transformation.

Down

1. A cold-blooded vertebrate that lives in water, breathes through gills, and is characterized by its scales and fins.

3. A powerful carnivorous feline with distinctive stripes, known for its agility, stealth, and remarkable hunting skills.

5. A large carnivorous feline with a majestic mane, often considered the king of the jungle and known for its strength, pride, and hunting prowess.

7. A large, hoofed mammal with a flowing mane and tail, often used for riding, racing, or working purposes and known for its strength and grace.

8. A domesticated mammal that is often kept as a pet and is known for its loyalty, playfulness, and companionship.

9. A flightless bird that resides in cold regions, characterized by its black and white feathers, waddling walk, and its skill at swimming underwater.

12. A small, furry mammal with long ears and a fluffy tail, often kept as a pet and known for its hopping and eating habits.

15. A feathered creature that possesses the ability to fly, often known for its beautiful plumage, diverse species, and melodious songs.

Body

Across

3. A muscular organ in the mouth responsible for tasting, swallowing, and speaking. The tongue helps manipulate food during chewing, forms sounds for speech, and contains taste buds that detect different flavors.

4. The muscular organ that pumps blood throughout the body. The heart is located in the chest and is responsible for supplying oxygen and nutrients to the tissues and organs, ensuring their proper functioning.

6. The outer covering of the body that protects internal organs and tissues. The skin acts as a barrier against harmful substances, regulates body temperature, and contains sensory receptors for touch and pain.

7. The opening in the face used for eating, speaking, and expressing emotions. The mouth contains teeth, a tongue, and salivary glands, and it serves as an entrance to the digestive and respiratory systems.

9. The facial organ used for breathing and smelling. The nose contains nostrils through which air is inhaled and exhaled, and it houses olfactory receptors that detect and distinguish various scents and odors.

11. The front part of the head that includes the eyes, nose, mouth, and other facial features.

Down

1. The terminal part of the leg that comes into contact with the ground. Feet provide support, balance, and locomotion, enabling walking, running, and jumping.

2. The lower limb of the body that supports standing, walking, and running. Legs consist of the thigh, knee, shin, and foot and allow for mobility and balance.

4. The part of the body attached to the end of the arm, consisting of the palm, fingers, and thumb. Hands are used for gripping, grasping, manipulating objects, and performing intricate tasks with fine motor skills.

5. The upper limb of the body extending from the shoulder to the hand. Arms are used for various tasks, such as reaching, grasping, and manipulating objects, and they are connected to the torso through the shoulder joint.

6. An organ located in the abdomen that receives and breaks down food through the process of digestion. The stomach secretes digestive juices and acids to chemically break down food before it moves to the intestines.

8. Hard structures in the mouth used for biting, chewing, and grinding food. Teeth are firmly rooted in the jawbone and come in different

The face is associated with expressions, emotions, and sensory functions such as vision, smell, and taste.

12. The uppermost part of the body that contains the brain, eyes, nose, mouth, and other sensory organs. The head sits on top of the neck and is responsible for housing and protecting the brain and facilitating various senses.

14. The central organ of the nervous system and the control center of the body. The brain processes sensory information, controls thoughts and emotions, and coordinates body movements and functions.

shapes and sizes, with different types serving specific functions in the mouth.

10. The organ responsible for vision. Eyes detect light and convert it into electrical signals that the brain interprets as visual information. People have two eyes, allowing for depth perception and a wider field of view.

13. The organ responsible for hearing and balance. Ears capture sound waves and transmit them to the brain for interpretation. They also play a role in maintaining equilibrium and spatial orientation.

Books

Across

4. A long work of fiction, usually in prose form, that tells a story and explores characters, settings, and events in depth.

5. A reference book that lists words alphabetically and provides definitions, spellings, and other language information.

8. A written account of someone's life, usually written by another person and covering various

Down

1. Book A book that provides information or specific facts on a particular subject, often used for consultation or research purposes.

2. A personal record of thoughts, experiences, or observations, often written on a regular basis.

3. A comprehensive reference work that provides information and explanations on various subjects or branches of knowledge.

aspects of their personal and professional experiences.

10. A written account of a person's own life, in which they reflect on their experiences, memories, and achievements.

13. Prose writing that presents factual information or discusses real events, ideas, or people.

15. Book A book that tells a story primarily through illustrations, often aimed at young children.

16. A personal narrative that focuses on specific experiences, memories, or periods in the author's life.

6. A book used as a standard source of information and instruction in a particular subject or field, often used in educational settings.

7. A book containing a collection of stories, often intended for children and accompanied by illustrations.

9. A periodical publication that contains articles, stories, photographs, and other written or visual content.

11. Literary work in which language is used for its aesthetic qualities, rhythm, and emotional expression, often employing metrical and imaginative techniques.

12. A collection of printed or written pages bound together, typically with a cover, containing stories, information, or pictures.

14. Imaginative or invented stories, often characterized by elements of creativity, imagination, and narrative.

Buildings

Across

1. A building that showcases art, artifacts, or exhibitions for educational and cultural purposes. Museums preserve and display objects of historical, scientific, or artistic significance for public viewing.

3. A place of worship for Christians. Churches are often characterized by their distinctive architecture and serve as gathering places for religious ceremonies, prayers, and community activities.

6. An establishment that provides temporary accommodations for travelers and tourists. Hotels offer rooms or suites for overnight stays, along with services such as room service, restaurants, and recreational facilities.

7. A place where students go to learn and receive education. Schools have classrooms, libraries, playgrounds, and other facilities that support teaching and learning.

Down

2. A place where goods or services are sold to customers. Stores can include grocery stores, clothing stores, bookstores, and more, and they typically have a designated area for browsing and making purchases.

4. A residential building where people live. Houses can vary in size and style, and they typically have rooms for different purposes such as bedrooms, living rooms, kitchens, and bathrooms.

5. A facility where people receive medical treatment and care. Hospitals have various departments, including emergency rooms, operating rooms, and patient rooms, and they are staffed by medical professionals.

8. A building that houses collections of books and other resources for reading, studying, and research. Libraries often have quiet areas, reading rooms, and computer facilities for visitors to access information.

11. A place where people work, usually in a professional or business setting. Offices can be found in commercial buildings and provide workspace for individuals or groups engaged in administrative tasks.

13. An extremely tall building with multiple floors, typically found in urban areas. Skyscrapers are known for their impressive height and architectural design, often housing offices, hotels, or residential units.

14. A building or part of a building that contains multiple residential units. Apartments are often rented or owned by individuals or families and offer separate living spaces within a larger building.

9. A financial institution where people can deposit money, withdraw cash, and conduct various financial transactions. Banks have teller windows, ATMs, and private offices for customers to manage their finances.

10. Office A facility where postal services such as mail collection, sorting, and delivery are conducted. Post offices provide mailboxes, postage services, and shipping options for individuals and businesses.

12. A building where goods are manufactured or produced on a large scale. Factories contain machinery, assembly lines, and production areas for various industries, such as automotive, textile, or electronics.

13. A large venue for sports, concerts, and other events. Stadiums have seating for spectators, playing fields, stages, and facilities for concessions and restrooms to accommodate large crowds.

Cities

Across

4. An area of land set aside for public recreation and enjoyment within a city. Parks may feature green spaces, trees, playgrounds, sports facilities, walking paths, and picnic areas, providing a place for relaxation, exercise, and socializing amidst the urban environment.

6. A residential area located on the outskirts of a city, typically characterized by single-family homes, quieter streets, and a more suburban lifestyle. Suburbs provide a balance between urban amenities and a quieter living environment.

8. The art and science of designing and constructing buildings and other physical structures. Architecture shapes the visual character and aesthetics of a city, encompassing a wide range of styles, materials, and techniques used in the creation of urban spaces.

10. A notable or significant feature, monument, building, or structure that is easily recognizable and serves as a point of reference or historical importance within a city. Landmarks contribute to a city's identity, cultural heritage, and tourist attractions.

13. A wide and often tree-lined road or street, typically running through the center of a city or

Down

1. A structure built to span physical obstacles such as rivers, canals, or valleys, providing a passage over the obstacle. Bridges connect different parts of a city, facilitating transportation and enhancing connectivity between neighborhoods and areas separated by natural or artificial barriers.

2. A designated area or building where goods, produce, or merchandise are sold, often featuring a variety of vendors and stalls. Markets are vibrant and bustling places within a city, offering fresh food, local products, crafts, and a vibrant atmosphere of trade and interaction.

3. An extremely tall building with multiple floors, typically found in cities. Skyscrapers are architectural icons that dominate the city skyline and house offices, residential units, hotels, or other commercial establishments. They are a symbol of urban modernity and progress.

5. An open public square or pedestrian area in the heart of a city, often surrounded by buildings, shops, restaurants, and other amenities. Plazas serve as gathering places, venues for events and performances, and focal

a prominent area. Avenues are known for their grandeur, architectural landmarks, high-end shops, and significant urban intersections. They often serve as major transportation routes.

14. A specific area or community within a city, often characterized by its unique features, demographics, and social dynamics. Neighborhoods can vary in terms of their architecture, culture, amenities, and sense of community.

15. A large and highly populated urban area that serves as a center of commerce, culture, and government. Cities are characterized by their skyscrapers, residential neighborhoods, transportation networks, and various amenities such as parks, museums, shopping centers, and entertainment venues.

16. The distinctive outline or silhouette of a city's buildings and structures against the sky, often seen from a distance or elevated viewpoint. A city's skyline is a prominent visual feature and may be recognizable and iconic.

points of social and cultural activities within the urban landscape.

7. Relating to or characteristic of a city or urban area. Urban environments are typically densely populated and offer a wide range of facilities, services, and opportunities for social, cultural, and economic activities.

9. The movement of vehicles, pedestrians, and other modes of transportation on roads and streets within a city. Traffic is often a significant aspect of urban life and can vary in intensity, congestion, and flow depending on the time of day and location.

11. The central business district of a city, usually characterized by tall buildings, offices, commercial establishments, and bustling activity. Downtown areas are often the economic and cultural hubs of a city, featuring shops, restaurants, theaters, and other attractions.

12. Transportation The system of transportation available to the general public within a city, including buses, trains, trams, subways, and other forms of mass transit. Public transportation provides a convenient and often more sustainable alternative to private vehicles for commuting and getting around the city.

Buildings

Across

1. A building that showcases art, artifacts, or exhibitions for educational and cultural purposes. Museums preserve and display objects of historical, scientific, or artistic significance for public viewing.

3. A place of worship for Christians. Churches are often characterized by their distinctive architecture and serve as gathering places for religious ceremonies, prayers, and community activities.

6. An establishment that provides temporary accommodations for travelers and tourists. Hotels offer rooms or suites for overnight stays, along with services such as room service, restaurants, and recreational facilities.

7. A place where students go to learn and receive education. Schools have classrooms, libraries, playgrounds, and other facilities that support teaching and learning.

Down

2. A place where goods or services are sold to customers. Stores can include grocery stores, clothing stores, bookstores, and more, and they typically have a designated area for browsing and making purchases.

4. A residential building where people live. Houses can vary in size and style, and they typically have rooms for different purposes such as bedrooms, living rooms, kitchens, and bathrooms.

5. A facility where people receive medical treatment and care. Hospitals have various departments, including emergency rooms, operating rooms, and patient rooms, and they are staffed by medical professionals.

8. A building that houses collections of books and other resources for reading, studying, and research. Libraries often have quiet areas, reading rooms, and computer facilities for visitors to access information.

11. A place where people work, usually in a professional or business setting. Offices can be found in commercial buildings and provide workspace for individuals or groups engaged in administrative tasks.

13. An extremely tall building with multiple floors, typically found in urban areas. Skyscrapers are known for their impressive height and architectural design, often housing offices, hotels, or residential units.

14. A building or part of a building that contains multiple residential units. Apartments are often rented or owned by individuals or families and offer separate living spaces within a larger building.

9. A financial institution where people can deposit money, withdraw cash, and conduct various financial transactions. Banks have teller windows, ATMs, and private offices for customers to manage their finances.

10. Office A facility where postal services such as mail collection, sorting, and delivery are conducted. Post offices provide mailboxes, postage services, and shipping options for individuals and businesses.

12. A building where goods are manufactured or produced on a large scale. Factories contain machinery, assembly lines, and production areas for various industries, such as automotive, textile, or electronics.

13. A large venue for sports, concerts, and other events. Stadiums have seating for spectators, playing fields, stages, and facilities for concessions and restrooms to accommodate large crowds.

Cities

Across

4. An area of land set aside for public recreation and enjoyment within a city. Parks may feature green spaces, trees, playgrounds, sports facilities, walking paths, and picnic areas, providing a place for relaxation, exercise, and socializing amidst the urban environment.

6. A residential area located on the outskirts of a city, typically characterized by single-family homes, quieter streets, and a more suburban lifestyle. Suburbs provide a balance between urban amenities and a quieter living environment.

8. The art and science of designing and constructing buildings and other physical structures. Architecture shapes the visual character and aesthetics of a city, encompassing a wide range of styles, materials, and techniques used in the creation of urban spaces.

10. A notable or significant feature, monument, building, or structure that is easily recognizable and serves as a point of reference or historical importance within a city. Landmarks contribute to a city's identity, cultural heritage, and tourist attractions.

13. A wide and often tree-lined road or street, typically running through the center of a city or

Down

1. A structure built to span physical obstacles such as rivers, canals, or valleys, providing a passage over the obstacle. Bridges connect different parts of a city, facilitating transportation and enhancing connectivity between neighborhoods and areas separated by natural or artificial barriers.

2. A designated area or building where goods, produce, or merchandise are sold, often featuring a variety of vendors and stalls. Markets are vibrant and bustling places within a city, offering fresh food, local products, crafts, and a vibrant atmosphere of trade and interaction.

3. An extremely tall building with multiple floors, typically found in cities. Skyscrapers are architectural icons that dominate the city skyline and house offices, residential units, hotels, or other commercial establishments. They are a symbol of urban modernity and progress.

5. An open public square or pedestrian area in the heart of a city, often surrounded by buildings, shops, restaurants, and other amenities. Plazas serve as gathering places, venues for events and performances, and focal

a prominent area. Avenues are known for their grandeur, architectural landmarks, high-end shops, and significant urban intersections. They often serve as major transportation routes.

14. A specific area or community within a city, often characterized by its unique features, demographics, and social dynamics. Neighborhoods can vary in terms of their architecture, culture, amenities, and sense of community.

15. A large and highly populated urban area that serves as a center of commerce, culture, and government. Cities are characterized by their skyscrapers, residential neighborhoods, transportation networks, and various amenities such as parks, museums, shopping centers, and entertainment venues.

16. The distinctive outline or silhouette of a city's buildings and structures against the sky, often seen from a distance or elevated viewpoint. A city's skyline is a prominent visual feature and may be recognizable and iconic.

points of social and cultural activities within the urban landscape.

7. Relating to or characteristic of a city or urban area. Urban environments are typically densely populated and offer a wide range of facilities, services, and opportunities for social, cultural, and economic activities.

9. The movement of vehicles, pedestrians, and other modes of transportation on roads and streets within a city. Traffic is often a significant aspect of urban life and can vary in intensity, congestion, and flow depending on the time of day and location.

11. The central business district of a city, usually characterized by tall buildings, offices, commercial establishments, and bustling activity. Downtown areas are often the economic and cultural hubs of a city, featuring shops, restaurants, theaters, and other attractions.

12. Transportation The system of transportation available to the general public within a city, including buses, trains, trams, subways, and other forms of mass transit. Public transportation provides a convenient and often more sustainable alternative to private vehicles for commuting and getting around the city.

Clothes

Across

3. A long, narrow piece of fabric worn around the neck or shoulders for warmth or fashion. It can be made of various materials and come in different patterns and styles.

5. Casual shoes with rubber soles, typically used for sports or everyday activities. They are comfortable and provide support for the feet.

7. A head covering worn for protection, fashion, or ceremonial purposes. It can have a brim or be without one.

8. A knitted garment worn on the upper body, typically with long sleeves. It is designed to provide warmth and can be made of wool, cotton, or synthetic fibers.

9. A heavy outer garment worn for warmth, typically extending below the waist and having a collar and buttons or a zipper. It is often made of wool or other warm fabrics.

10. A one-piece garment for women or girls that covers the body and extends down the legs. It is typically worn for formal or dressy occasions and can be made of various styles and fabrics.

12. A casual garment with short sleeves and a round or V-shaped neckline. It is typically made

Down

1. Garments worn on the feet, covering the ankles and lower legs. They are usually made of cotton or wool and come in various lengths and thicknesses.

2. A garment worn on the upper body, typically with long sleeves and buttons or a zipper at the front. It is usually worn as outerwear and can be made of various fabrics and styles.

3. A garment worn by women or girls, hanging from the waist and covering the lower body. It is typically shorter than a dress and can be made of various lengths and materials.

4. A garment worn on the lower body, covering both legs separately. It typically has a waistband, a fly with buttons or a zipper, and may have pockets.

6. A garment worn on the upper body, usually with short or long sleeves and buttons or a zipper at the front. It covers the torso and can be made of various fabrics.

8. Open-toed footwear that consists of a sole and straps or thongs. They are typically worn in warm weather and allow the feet to breathe.

11. A garment worn on the lower body, covering the hips and upper thighs. It is typically shorter

of cotton and worn on the upper body.

13. Hand coverings worn to keep the hands warm and provide protection. They typically cover the fingers and may extend to the wrist.

than pants and can be made of various materials.

Colors

Across

3. A metallic color that is often associated with modernity, sophistication, and high-tech.

7. A vibrant color that is often associated with calmness, clarity, and communication.

8. A dark color that is often associated with mystery, elegance, and power.

9. A earthy color that is often associated with stability, reliability, and warmth.

11. A refreshing color that is often associated with nature, growth, and harmony.

13. A bright color that is often associated with happiness, joy, and optimism.

14. A vibrant color that is often associated with love, passion, and energy.

Down

1. A bold color that is often associated with creativity, individuality, and self-expression.

2. A pure color that is often associated with innocence, purity, and simplicity.

4. A warm color that is often associated with enthusiasm, creativity, and adventure.

5. A royal color that is often associated with luxury, mystery, and spirituality.

6. A delicate color that is often associated with femininity, tenderness, and sweetness.

9. A calming color that is often associated with serenity, tranquility, and a sense of peace.

10. A neutral color that is often associated with balance, maturity, and practicality.

12. A precious color that is often associated with luxury, wealth, and success.

Countries

Across

3. A political entity with its own government and internal affairs.

5. A country ruled by a king or queen.

7. A political association of states with shared goals and interests.

8. A self-governing territory within the British Empire.

10. A group of territories ruled by an emperor or empress.

12. A division of a country or region with its own administration.

Down

1. A large group of people who share the same language and culture.

2. A nation where the citizens hold the power and choose their leaders.

4. The country or region where someone has their roots or heritage.

6. A specific territory or geographic area.

7. A union or alliance of states or regions with shared interests.

9. An area of land governed by a specific country or ruling power.

13. A place with its own government, borders, and distinct culture.

14. The status of being an independent political entity.

11. Having the power to govern oneself and make independent decisions.

Experiences

Across

3. The act of carefully watching or examining something in order to gain information.

6. A scientific or systematic test conducted to acquire knowledge or validate a hypothesis.

Down

1. The act of trying out new ideas, methods, or approaches in order to learn and discover.

2. The process of communication or engagement between individuals or objects.

8. The act of finding or uncovering something for the first time.

10. A short trip or outing, usually for leisure, educational, or recreational purposes.

13. The process of investigating or discovering new places, ideas, or activities.

14. The act of deeply engaging or involving oneself in a particular experience or activity.

15. A remarkable or intense experience that affects the senses and evokes strong feelings.

16. A meeting or experience with someone or something, often unexpectedly.

4. The act of carefully watching or examining something in order to gain information.

5. A display or presentation of skills, talents, or abilities in front of an audience.

7. The act of taking part in or being involved in an activity, event, or process.

9. An exciting experience or journey that involves taking risks or exploring new places.

11. A task or situation that tests one's abilities, skills, or determination.

12. A journey or search undertaken in order to achieve a specific goal or find something valuable.

Fairy Tales

Across

3. The ability to create mental images, ideas, or concepts that are not present in reality.

6. A book containing a collection of stories, often illustrated and aimed at children.

9. tale A fictional story that typically features magical elements, enchanted characters, and a moral lesson.

10. An exciting and daring experience or journey, often involving heroic characters.

12. Stories from the past that are based on historical events but often contain mythical or

Down

1. A genre of literature that involves elements of magic, supernatural beings, and imaginary worlds.

2. Traditional stories, customs, and beliefs passed down through generations by a specific culture or community.

4. Relating to myths or legendary stories, often involving gods, goddesses, and extraordinary creatures.

5. Inspiring a sense of wonder and amazement, often associated with magical or extraordinary elements.

exaggerated elements.

15. A small imaginary being with magical powers, often depicted as having wings and associated with nature.

16. The people, animals, or creatures who appear in the story and play a role in the narrative.

7. A journey or expedition undertaken by a character in a story, usually to achieve a specific goal.

8. The lesson or ethical principle conveyed by a story, often aimed at teaching values.

11. Under the spell or influence of magic, often resulting in a transformed or extraordinary state.

13. The feeling of being captivated or charmed by something magical or fantastical.

14. Existing only in the imagination or fantasy, not in reality.

Family

Across

4. A relative who is the child of one's aunt or uncle, often around the same age, providing a special connection, shared experiences, and familial camaraderie.

5. A young person who is a son or daughter, the cherished and loved member of a family, filled with curiosity, imagination, and the promise of a bright future.

8. A person who becomes a parent through marriage to one's biological parent, providing love, care, and support, building a unique family dynamic and connection.

9. A group of people who are connected by blood or love, living together and supporting one another, sharing joys, sorrows, and experiences of life.

11. A brother or sister, a member of the same family, who shares common parents and often

Down

1. The sister of one's parent, who offers care, support, and guidance, often playing a special role in a child's life by providing love and affection.

2. The brother of one's parent, who serves as a role model, mentor, and source of guidance, offering support, wisdom, and a sense of fun and adventure.

3. The daughter of one's sibling or sibling-in-law, a special young girl who brings joy, laughter, and a sense of wonder to the family with her youthful energy.

6. A person who is married to one's sibling, bringing new connections and relationships to the family, often developing strong bonds and becoming like a blood relative.

7. A step-brother or step-sister, a person who becomes a sibling through the marriage of one's

develops a lifelong bond of friendship and companionship.

13. A person who is legally responsible for the care and well-being of a child, offering protection, support, and guidance when the child's parents are unable to do so.

14. The son of one's sibling or sibling-in-law, a beloved young boy who brings excitement, mischief, and a sense of playfulness to the family dynamic.

15. parent A person who cares for a child temporarily, providing a safe and nurturing home environment, love, and support, while the child's biological family situation is resolved.

parent, creating a blended family with new relationships and connections.

10. A grandmother or grandfather, the parents of one's own parents, who shower their grandchildren with love, wisdom, and cherished memories from their own lives.

12. A mother or father who takes care of a child, providing love, guidance, and support, teaching them valuable lessons and helping them grow into responsible adults.

Flowers

Across

2. Simple flower with white petals and yellow center.

3. Beautiful and colorful plant with petals.

6. Colorful flower with delicate, papery petals.

7. Exotic flower known for its intricate beauty.

10. Delicate flower with trumpet-shaped petals.

12. Fragrant flower often used in bouquets and arrangements.

13. Graceful flower with cup-shaped blooms.

14. Small flower with purple or blue petals.

Down

1. Large, showy flower with layered petals.

2. Bright yellow flower with a trumpet-shaped center.

4. Fragrant flower with thorny stems.

5. Fragrant flower known for its clustered blooms.

8. Tall plant with large yellow flower head.

9. Vibrant flower often seen in orange and yellow hues.

11. Elegant flower with vibrant and varied colors.

Food

Across

2. A sweet and fluffy breakfast treat made from a batter of flour, milk, and eggs, usually served with syrup, butter, or fruit toppings.

5. A versatile food made from unleavened dough that is rolled flat and cut into thin strips, typically cooked and served in a broth.

6. A delicious dish made with a thin, crispy crust topped with cheese, tomato sauce, and various toppings of your choice.

8. A sweet and fluffy breakfast treat made from a batter of flour, milk, and eggs, usually served with syrup, butter, or fruit toppings.

9. A healthy dish made with a combination of fresh vegetables, fruits, and sometimes proteins like chicken or tuna, served with dressing.

Down

1. A popular Italian dish made from noodles, usually served with a variety of sauces, such as marinara, Alfredo, or carbonara.

3. A versatile food made from unleavened dough that is rolled flat and cut into thin strips, typically cooked and served in a broth.

4. A delicious dish made with a thin, crispy crust topped with cheese, tomato sauce, and various toppings of your choice.

7. A convenient meal made by placing various ingredients, such as meat, cheese, and vegetables, between two slices of bread.

9. A comforting dish made by simmering ingredients, such as vegetables, meat, or legumes, in a flavorful broth or stock.

10. A comforting dish made by simmering ingredients, such as vegetables, meat, or legumes, in a flavorful broth or stock.

11. cream A frozen dessert made from dairy products, sugar, and various flavors, enjoyed in a cone, cup, or as a topping for other desserts.

13. A traditional Japanese dish consisting of bite-sized portions of raw or cooked fish, seafood, or vegetables served with rice.

15. A tasty sandwich consisting of a grilled or fried patty made from ground meat, typically beef, served in a bun with toppings.

12. A tasty sandwich consisting of a grilled or fried patty made from ground meat, typically beef, served in a bun with toppings.

14. cream A frozen dessert made from dairy products, sugar, and various flavors, enjoyed in a cone, cup, or as a topping for other desserts.

Fruits

Across

4. A soft, fuzzy fruit with a round shape and a yellow or reddish skin. It has a sweet and juicy flesh and is often enjoyed fresh or used in pies, preserves, and desserts.

5. Small, red berries with a sweet and slightly tart flavor. They have a soft texture and are commonly eaten fresh, used in desserts, or made into jams and sauces.

6. A large, juicy fruit with a green rind and sweet, red or pink flesh. It is typically eaten in slices and is refreshing, especially during hot summer days.

8. A juicy fruit with a smooth, orange skin and sweet, tropical taste. It has a fibrous flesh

Down

1. A long, curved fruit with a yellow peel. It has a soft, sweet flesh and is commonly consumed as a snack or added to desserts and smoothies.

2. A fruit with a distinctive shape, usually narrow at the top and wider at the bottom. It has a smooth, thin skin and a crisp, juicy flesh. Pears are eaten fresh or used in cooking.

3. A round or oval-shaped fruit with a firm and juicy flesh. It typically has a red or green skin and is often eaten fresh or used in various dishes.

7. A citrus fruit with a bright orange color and a sweet, tangy flavor. It is often peeled and eaten fresh or used to make juice.

surrounding a large, flat pit and is commonly eaten fresh or used in smoothies and salsas.

10. Small, round berries with a dark blue or purple skin. They have a sweet and slightly tart taste and are commonly eaten fresh or used in baked goods, jams, and smoothies.

13. A small, round fruit with a bright red or dark purple skin. It has a sweet and tart flavor and a hard pit in the center. Cherries are often eaten fresh or used in desserts.

15. A tropical fruit with a rough, spiky skin and sweet, yellow flesh. It has a tangy flavor and is often consumed fresh or used in tropical dishes and desserts.

9. Small, round fruits that grow in clusters on vines. Grapes can be green, red, or purple and are enjoyed fresh or used to make wine, juices, and jams.

11. A citrus fruit with a bright yellow, acidic flesh and a sour taste. It is often used to add flavor to foods and beverages, such as lemonade, salads, and desserts.

12. A small, juicy fruit with a red, textured skin and small seeds on the surface. It has a sweet and slightly tart taste and is popular in desserts and as a topping.

14. A small, oval-shaped fruit with a brown, fuzzy skin and green flesh. It has a tangy and sweet flavor and is typically eaten fresh or used in fruit salads and smoothies.

Hobbies

Across

3. Physical activities or games that require skill, athleticism, and competition, such as soccer, basketball, swimming, or tennis, providing opportunities for exercise and teamwork.

4. The activity of expressing thoughts, ideas, or stories through written words, often involving creative storytelling, journaling, or composing essays.

6. The activity of cultivating and tending to plants, flowers, or a garden, involving tasks such as planting, watering, and pruning.

10. The activity of gathering and acquiring a specific type of objects or items based on personal interest or hobby, such as stamps, coins, or trading cards.

Down

1. The process of preparing food by combining ingredients, following recipes, and utilizing culinary techniques to create delicious meals or dishes.

2. The act of solving puzzles, brain teasers, or challenging games that require logic, problem-solving, and critical thinking skills to reach a solution or complete a task.

3. The skill or practice of using a needle and thread to join or create garments, accessories, or fabric items, often involving techniques like stitching, hemming, or embroidering.

5. The act of applying color or pigments to a surface using brushes, fingers, or other tools to create artwork or express creativity.

11. The act of interpreting and comprehending written text, books, or literature, often for entertainment, learning, or expanding knowledge.

12. Music The act of creating and performing music using instruments or one's voice, often involving skills like playing an instrument, singing, or composing songs.

13. The art or practice of moving rhythmically to music, expressing emotions or storytelling through bodily movements, often involving various dance styles or choreography.

7. The art or practice of capturing and producing images using a camera, often to document moments, express creativity, or convey a message.

8. An activity or interest pursued for pleasure, relaxation, or personal enjoyment during one's free time.

9. The act of creating images, patterns, or representations on a surface using various tools such as pencils, pens, or charcoal.

14. The practice of making handmade objects or artwork using various materials such as paper, fabric, wood, or beads, often involving skills like sewing, knitting, or woodworking.

Housing

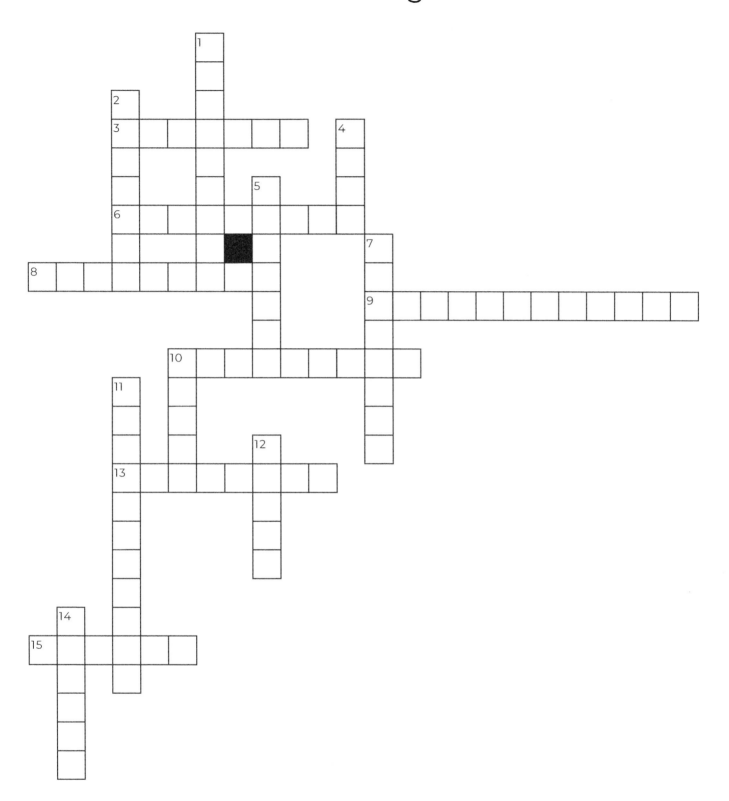

Across

3. The natural environment or surroundings in which a particular species or community of organisms lives.

6. A tall, narrow house with multiple floors, typically sharing walls with neighboring houses.

8. A self-contained unit within a larger building, typically consisting of several rooms and used

Down

1. A place where someone lives, such as a house, apartment, or other dwelling.

2. A place providing protection and refuge, often for those without a permanent home.

4. A place where someone lives and feels a sense of belonging, comfort, and security.

as a residence.

9. A specific area or community where people live and interact with one another.

10. A house and the surrounding land, typically used for agricultural purposes or as a family residence.

13. A place of residence, where people live or stay.

15. A residential area located on the outskirts of a city or town, typically characterized by houses and a quieter atmosphere.

5. A small, cozy house, often located in a rural or scenic area.

7. A one-story house with a low-pitched roof, often surrounded by a porch or veranda.

10. A building where people live, usually with rooms for sleeping, cooking, and other activities.

11. A multi-unit property where each unit is individually owned, while common areas are shared among residents.

12. A large and luxurious house, often located in a desirable or picturesque setting.

14. A building divided into two separate residential units, each with its own entrance.

Industries

Across

2. Systematic investigation or study conducted to gain knowledge, insights, or solutions to scientific, technical, or industrial problems.

Down

1. The process of creating, improving, or advancing products, technologies, or

3. The use of technology and machines to control and operate industrial processes, reducing the need for human intervention.

5. The introduction of new ideas, methods, technologies, or products that lead to improvements, advancements, or changes within an industry.

6. The production of goods or services within an economy, typically involving manufacturing, mining, or technology sectors.

9. The practice of conducting industrial activities in a way that meets present needs without compromising the ability of future generations to meet their own needs.

10. Mechanical devices or equipment used in manufacturing, production, or other industrial processes to perform specific tasks or functions.

12. A building or facility where goods are produced or manufactured using machinery, equipment, and a labor force.

14. The ability to accomplish a task or produce desired outputs with minimal waste, time, effort, or resources in an industrial context.

15. Chain The network of organizations, resources, activities, and processes involved in the production, distribution, and delivery of goods or services.

16. The management and coordination of the flow of goods, information, and resources within a supply chain, from the point of origin to consumption.

infrastructure to meet specific needs or objectives.

4. The process of transforming raw materials or components into finished products through various production techniques and methods.

7. The process of starting, managing, and organizing a business or venture, often involving innovation, risk-taking, and resource management in an industrial context.

8. A large industrial facility or complex where various operations, such as manufacturing, processing, or refining, take place.

11. The creation, assembly, or manufacturing of goods or services for commercial purposes using resources, labor, and technology.

13. Line A manufacturing process in which a product is assembled sequentially by workers stationed along a conveyor belt or production line.

Landmarks

Across

2. A large area of land preserved for recreational and aesthetic purposes, often featuring natural beauty, green spaces, and facilities for outdoor activities.

4. A famous or important feature or structure in a city or region that is easily recognized and serves as a symbol of that place.

5. A large fortified building or structure with historical and architectural significance, often associated with medieval times and royalty.

Down

1. A structure built to span physical obstacles such as rivers, ravines, or valleys, providing passage for vehicles, pedestrians, or trains.

3. An area of land cultivated with plants, flowers, and trees, often designed for aesthetic pleasure, relaxation, and enjoyment of nature.

6. A place, event, or activity that is interesting, enjoyable, and draws the attention of visitors or tourists.

7. A grand residence or official building, typically associated with royalty or high-ranking officials, known for its architectural beauty and historical significance.

8. A facility where aquatic animals, plants, and ecosystems are displayed and studied, providing an opportunity to learn about marine life and conservation.

9. A large venue or facility designed for sports events, concerts, or other performances, typically with seating for a large audience.

10. A location equipped with telescopes and other instruments for observing celestial objects, such as stars, planets, and galaxies.

12. Park A theme park that offers a variety of attractions, rides, and entertainment for people of all ages, creating a fun and thrilling experience.

11. A large and important Christian church that serves as the central place of worship for a diocese, known for its grandeur and religious significance.

15. A structure, statue, or building that is built to commemorate a person, event, or historical significance and often holds cultural or symbolic value.

13. A place where objects of artistic, cultural, historical, or scientific importance are preserved, exhibited, and studied for public viewing and education.

16. A tower-like structure equipped with a bright light that serves as a navigational aid and warning to ships, especially in coastal areas.

14. A facility where various species of animals are kept for public display, observation, and conservation purposes.

Music

Across

2. The words of a song or the text that is sung.

5. A device used to create music, such as a piano or guitar.

7. Sounds and rhythms arranged in a pleasing way.

9. A catchy and memorable melody or musical phrase.

11. A group of musicians who play instruments and perform together.

13. A live presentation or execution of music in front of an audience.

15. The combination of different musical sounds played together.

Down

1. The person who leads and directs an orchestra or choir.

3. The pattern of strong and weak beats in music.

4. A group of singers who perform together.

6. A large group of musicians who play different instruments together.

8. The speed at which music is played or sung.

10. A piece of music with lyrics that is sung.

11. The steady pulse or rhythm in music that you can tap your foot to.

12. A single sound in music, represented by a symbol on sheet music.

14. A sequence of musical notes that create a tuneful line.

Nature

Across

2. A large body of water surrounded by land. It is often freshwater and can provide habitat for various aquatic plants and animals.

7. A cascade of water falling from a height, often found in rivers or streams. It creates a beautiful and relaxing natural sight.

9. The natural satellite of the Earth, which orbits around it and reflects light from the Sun.

10. The star at the center of the solar system, which provides heat and light to Earth.

11. A tall plant with a woody stem, branches, and leaves. It provides shade, produces oxygen, and can bear fruits or flowers.

12. The reproductive structure found in plants. It typically has colorful petals and produces seeds.

14. A sandy or pebbly shore along the edge of a body of water, such as an ocean or a lake. It is a popular spot for relaxation.

Down

1. A luminous celestial body visible in the night sky, typically consisting of a mass of gas that emits light and heat.

3. The third planet from the Sun and the only known planet to support life. It has a diverse environment with land, water, and air.

4. A large area of land covered with trees, plants, and wildlife. It is an important ecosystem and provides oxygen and habitat.

5. A meteorological phenomenon that forms a spectrum of colors in the sky. It occurs when sunlight is refracted and reflected by water droplets in the air.

6. A visible mass of water vapor suspended in the atmosphere. It can take different shapes and can bring rain or shade.

7. The natural movement of air, usually caused by differences in temperature and pressure. It can be gentle or strong.

8. A landform that rises high above its surroundings, typically with steep slopes and a pointed or rounded summit.

13. A large flowing body of water that moves towards a lake, sea, or ocean. It is formed by

streams and carries water and sediment.

Nouns

Across

2. A domesticated animal that is commonly kept as a pet. Dogs are known for their loyalty, companionship, and playful nature. They come in various breeds, sizes, and colors, and are often considered part of the family. They require care, including feeding, grooming, and exercise, and can provide comfort, love, and protection to their owners.

4. A written or printed work consisting of pages bound together. Books can contain stories, information, or pictures, and are a valuable source of knowledge, entertainment, and imagination. They come in different genres, such as fiction, non-fiction, and picture books. Reading books stimulates the mind, enhances vocabulary, and opens up new worlds and ideas.

5. The star at the center of the solar system that provides light, heat, and energy to the Earth. The sun is essential for life, influencing the weather, climate, and natural cycles. It appears as a bright, glowing ball in the sky during the day. The sun brings warmth, brightness, and a sense of awe, allowing plants to grow, creating shadows, and offering opportunities for outdoor activities.

Down

1. An electronic device that processes data and performs various tasks using programmed instructions. Computers are used for communication, information retrieval, creativity, and problem-solving. They consist of hardware components such as the monitor, keyboard, and mouse, and operate using software programs. Computers have revolutionized technology and play a vital role in modern society.

3. A building or structure that serves as a dwelling for people. Houses provide shelter, privacy, and a sense of belonging. They come in different styles, sizes, and architectural designs, reflecting cultural and regional influences. Houses consist of rooms, furniture, and amenities for living, and create a comfortable and secure environment for individuals and families.

6. A two-wheeled vehicle that is powered by pedals and used for transportation or recreational purposes. Bicycles are popular for exercise, commuting, and exploring the outdoors. They come in various styles, sizes, and colors, and can be adjusted to fit the rider's height. Riding a bicycle promotes physical

7. The art form of combining sounds, melodies, and rhythms to create expressive and harmonious compositions. Music can be performed using various instruments or through vocal techniques. It encompasses different genres, such as classical, pop, rock, and jazz, and is a source of entertainment, emotional expression, and cultural identity. Listening to music can evoke various emotions and enhance mood.

9. A motor vehicle with four wheels that is used for transportation. Cars come in different sizes, models, and colors, and are powered by internal combustion engines or electric motors. They provide convenience and mobility, allowing people to travel comfortably and quickly from one place to another. Cars require fuel and regular maintenance for optimal performance.

10. An object or device designed for play, enjoyment, and learning. Toys come in different forms, such as dolls, action figures, puzzles, and board games. They provide entertainment, stimulate creativity, and promote cognitive and motor skills development. Toys can be played with individually or with others, encouraging imagination, social interaction, and problem-solving abilities.

13. An optical device used to capture and record images and videos. Cameras can be digital or film-based and come in various types, such as DSLR, point-and-shoot, or smartphone cameras. They allow individuals to capture and preserve special moments, explore photography as a hobby or profession, and express their creativity through visual storytelling.

15. The reproductive structure of a plant, typically colorful and fragrant. Flowers come in various shapes, sizes, and colors and are often associated with beauty and symbolism. They are found in gardens, parks, and natural environments. Flowers attract pollinators and play a crucial role in plant reproduction, adding vibrancy and joy to the surroundings.

fitness, coordination, and a sense of freedom and adventure.

8. A small domesticated animal that is often kept as a pet. Cats are known for their independence, agility, and affectionate nature. They have a diverse range of breeds, sizes, and coat patterns. Cats are generally low-maintenance pets, requiring proper feeding, grooming, and a clean litter box. They provide companionship and can be playful and soothing to be around.

11. A designated area of land set aside for public recreation and enjoyment. Parks offer open spaces, playgrounds, trails, and natural environments for relaxation, exercise, and social activities. They can have features like benches, picnic areas, and sports facilities. Parks provide opportunities for outdoor activities, connecting people with nature and fostering a sense of community.

12. A spherical object used in various sports and games. Balls can be made of different materials such as rubber, leather, or plastic. They come in different sizes and are used for activities such as soccer, basketball, baseball, and tennis. Playing with balls promotes physical activity, coordination, and teamwork, providing hours of fun and enjoyment for individuals and groups.

14. A large perennial plant with a woody stem, branches, and leaves. Trees provide shade, oxygen, and habitats for various animals. They come in different species and can be found in forests, parks, and urban areas. Trees play a vital role in maintaining the ecological balance and are important for the environment and the overall well-being of the planet.

Numbers

Across

2. The number that represents a quantity of six or the sixth in a series. It is often represented by the symbol "6".

4. The number that represents a quantity of ten or the tenth in a series. It is often represented by the symbol "10".

6. The number that represents a quantity of thirteen. It is the sum of ten and three.

8. The number that represents a quantity of nine or the ninth in a series. It is often represented by the symbol "9".

9. The number that represents a quantity of four or the fourth in a series. It is often represented by the symbol "4".

11. The number that represents a quantity of twelve. It is the sum of ten and two.

13. The number that represents a quantity of five or the fifth in a series. It is often represented by the symbol "5".

14. The number that represents a quantity of fourteen. It is the sum of ten and four.

Down

1. The number that represents a quantity of eight or the eighth in a series. It is often represented by the symbol "8".

3. The number that represents a quantity of seven or the seventh in a series. It is often represented by the symbol "7".

5. The number that represents a quantity of eleven. It is the sum of ten and one.

6. The number that represents a quantity of three or the third in a series. It is often represented by the symbol "3".

7. The number that represents a quantity of fifteen. It is the sum of ten and five.

10. The number that represents a single unit or the first in a series. It is often represented by the symbol "1".

12. The number that represents a quantity of two or the second in a series. It is often represented by the symbol "2".